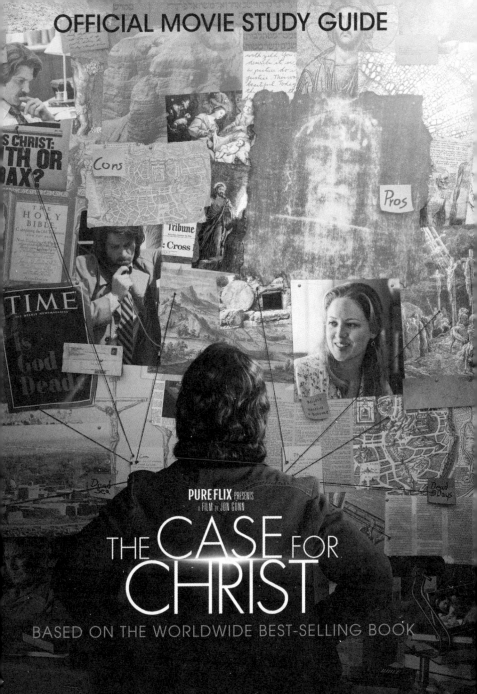

PURE FLIX PRESENTS

A FILM BY JON GUNN

THE CASE FOR CHRIST

BASED ON THE WORLDWIDE BEST-SELLING BOOK

The Case for Christ Study Guide
© 2017 by Outreach, Inc.

Published by Outreach, Inc., Colorado Springs, CO 80919

www.Outreach.com

ISBN: 9781635101300
Cover Design by Tim Downs
Interior Design by Alexia Garaventa
Executive Editor: Mark Mittelberg
Edited by Tia Smith
Contributing Author: Jeremy Jones

Printed in the United States of America

CONTENTS

FOREWORD

The Case for Christ is much more than just a book, a movie, or a series at a church. To my wife, Leslie, and me, it represents the information God used to revolutionize our lives, our marriage, our family, and our eternity.

That's why I'm so excited that you and your group will be gathering for four weeks to use this guide and talk about the important topics covered in the pages that follow. Regardless of where you're at in your spiritual journey, I believe the truths you'll discuss will point you to the God who loves you; bolster your confidence in the facts surrounding the ministry, death, and resurrection of God's Son, Jesus; motivate you to trust in him for his forgiveness and leadership in your life; and encourage you to spread his Good News to others.

If you're new to exploring spiritual matters, let me encourage you with the words of Jesus in Matthew 7:7–8: "Ask and it will be given to you; seek and you will find; knock and the door will be opened to you. For everyone who asks receives; the one who seeks finds; and to the one who knocks, the door will be opened." What a great promise! If you seriously pursue God, Jesus says, you will certainly find him.

And if you've been a Christian for some time, these discussions will help you heed the words of the apostle Peter in 1 Peter 3:15: "Always be prepared to give an answer to everyone who asks you to give the reason for the hope that you have. But do this with gentleness and respect." This study will aid you in knowing what you believe, why it makes sense, and how you can share it with others.

Ultimately, I believe God wants all of us to experience what Jesus described in John 8:32: "Then you will know the truth, and the truth will set you free."

To that end, you have my wholehearted prayers and encouragement!

LEE STROBEL
Author of *The Case for Christ*

INTRODUCTION

In 1980, Lee Strobel's award-winning investigative reporting earned him a promotion to legal editor at the *Chicago Tribune*. Things at home weren't going nearly as well. His wife Leslie's newfound faith in Christ compelled Lee to utilize his journalistic and legal training to disprove the claims of Christianity—pitting his resolute atheism against her growing faith.

Based on Strobel's best-selling book of the same name, *The Case for Christ* movie is a dramatic and heartfelt telling of Lee and Leslie's compelling journey. This book, *The Case for Christ Study Guide*, is a four-week study based on that movie. It will help the members of your group dig deeper into the evidence Lee Strobel uncovered and apply it to their own lives. Whether you're someone who is seeking spiritual truth, you're a new Christian, or you've been a believer for some time, this study provides an opportunity for you to find answers to the questions blocking your spiritual progress and growth.

It's been said that Jesus did not come into this world to make bad people good; he came into this world to make dead people alive. Over the next four weeks, may you find a new or renewed spiritual flame within yourself as you dig into *The Case for Christ Study Guide*.

HOW TO USE THIS STUDY GUIDE

This four-week study is designed to be interactive and accessible to individuals, small groups, and classes. Inspired by clips from *The Case for Christ* movie and rooted in Scripture, this study guide will help you take the next steps together in your journey with Christ. The four lessons cover these topics:

1. Investigating the Case for Christ

2. Exploring the Evidence for Christ

3. Embracing the Truth of Christ

4. Explaining the Good News of Christ

Small group leaders can refer to *The Case for Christ Leader's Guide* for specific instructions, available resources, and additional support on leading a small group. Each of the lessons has the following sections.

GET STARTED

Big Idea: A quick overview highlights the main theme of the lesson.

Icebreaker: A fun activity gets your group interacting, building relationships with one another while also tapping into the theme of the lesson.

WATCH

Video Clip: Each lesson connects to a relevant scene from the movie *The Case for Christ*.

Setup: A short description sets the stage for the scene and offers a bit of background info and a brief overview. This can be helpful to read before watching the video clip.

Recap: This section can help focus on the key themes or serve as a summary even if an individual or group isn't able to view the video at the time. It may be helpful to watch the video clip together before recapping here—or to revisit this description after viewing.

DISCUSS

The main course of the study, this section connects key lesson points and supporting Scripture with group discussion and personal reflection. Short examples and themes are interspersed with discussion questions to allow for an interactive time of group learning and discovery.

APPLY

Takeaway: A synopsis of the core lesson gives you a key truth to carry through your week.

Insights: This section provides a place to process and record personal thoughts and applications from the lesson.

Action: A challenge helps you apply throughout the week what was presented in the lesson. It's a reminder of insights gained and an opportunity to integrate God's work in and through your life.

Q&A WITH LEE STROBEL

At the end of each session is one question and answer session with Lee Strobel that relates to the theme of that week's lesson.

No. 651

Reporter's
Note Book

LESSON 1
Investigating the
Case for Christ

NOTES FROM _____ TO _____

GET STARTED

Big Idea: Connecting with God starts with seeking and exploring spiritual truth.

Icebreaker: Two Truths and a Lie

Go around the room, and have each group member tell three things about himself or herself. Two of the facts should be true, and one should be made up. After each person presents his or her three pieces of information, the group gets to vote on which ones were true and which one was fiction. Once everyone has taken a turn, talk about what made it easy or hard to determine the truth.

Which stories fooled everyone? Which truths were obvious? Why?

As we seek God and spiritual truth, there can be obstacles to our investigation, but the truth is always worth seeking.

WATCH

Video 1: Investigating the Case for Christ [DVD]

Setup: A young Lee Strobel sits at his desk in the newsroom. Tired and bleary-eyed, he is surrounded by books and notepads. Strobel has been engaged in a long, in-depth investigation to try to disprove Christianity and to liberate his wife, Leslie, from her newfound faith in Christ. He has read, researched, and talked to numerous experts, all in the age before the Internet. But he does not like the evidence he has uncovered or the answers it has continually

> "The heavens declare the glory of God; the skies proclaim the work of his hands. Day after day they pour forth speech; night after night they reveal knowledge. They have no speech, they use no words; no sound is heard from them. Yet their voice goes out into all the earth, their words to the ends of the world."
>
> —Psalm 19:1–4

pointed him toward. Strobel's coworker Kenny London, the *Chicago Tribune*'s religion editor, knows what this is all about. London realizes that this is more than a journalistic endeavor for Strobel—this investigation is personal.

Recap: It doesn't take long in this scene for London to sense that something is wrong with Strobel. When he asks, Strobel doesn't hold back from channeling all his frustration at London, peppering him with phrases like "you people and your God . . ." London has had enough. He stands up to Strobel, calling him out for his arrogance and his resistance to the facts he's uncovering. He challenges him to use his investigative skills to compare the evidence once and for all and make his call about the truth. "Stop blaming me and the church and God, and do your job," London blurts out. "Stack up the evidence, follow the facts, and write the story—win or lose!"

DISCUSS

Who do you identify with most in this scene: Lee Strobel or Kenny London? Why?

Kenny London paraphrases C. S. Lewis, saying, "If Christianity is false, it's of zero importance. But if it's true, there is nothing more important in the entire universe." How did that statement apply to Strobel's life? How does it apply to yours?

Read through each of the following lesson points and discuss the questions together.

1. Investigating Truth Is Worth It

Investigating spiritual truth and seeking reasons for what we believe are hard work. It can seem safer to rest on the beliefs of others or to paper over our doubts with shallow answers. Have you been there in your own life? Are you there now? The problem is that when we don't seek spiritual truth for ourselves, our faith can't flourish. When we fail to pursue truth and investigate what we believe and the evidence that supports it, our relationship with God and our faith in him have little or no foundation.

The good news is that the Bible is full of promises for those who seek spiritual truth. Even when it is difficult, the pursuit is worth it. Read these passages and discuss what they mean for you as you investigate Christ or seek a deeper faith in him:

> *Ask and it will be given to you; seek and you will find; knock and the door will be opened to you. For everyone who asks receives; the one who seeks finds; and to the one who knocks, the door will be opened. (Matthew 7:7–8)*

> *You will seek me and find me when you seek me with all your heart. (Jeremiah 29:13)*

What does it look like to believe and act upon these verses?

When have you seen these promises fulfilled in your own life, in your own pursuit of truth?

How are you asking, seeking, knocking, and waiting? What is your process, and how is it going?

2. Ask Hard Questions

As we've seen, God promises to meet us as we search for truth. But it's not always easy or comfortable, is it? In fact, as Christians we don't always put a lot of emphasis on the intellectual pursuit of truth. But Mark 12:30 tells us to "love the Lord your God with all your heart and with all your soul and with all your mind and with all your strength." Somehow, we often skip over the *mind* aspect of that verse. But it's key to investigating truth. And while it may seem counterintuitive, asking hard questions is often the start of loving God with our minds.

How do you usually dig deeper into something you want to know more about?

How can you apply that to your investigation of the truth about Christ?

What sources of information give you the most assurance of God's truth and existence?

A good investigator explores all the angles, and there are many ways to investigate God's truth. The Bible is a great place to start as it directly tells the story of God's love and salvation. History and science are other areas we should seek and encounter truth. These were vital parts of Lee Strobel's journey toward faith.

For some, the beauty, order, and wonder of nature serve as the strongest evidence of God's truth (Psalm 19:1–4). For others, the testimonies of changed lives are the strongest proof.

"Stop blaming me and the church and God, and do your job. Stack up the evidence, follow the facts, and write the story—win or lose!"

—Kenny London,
The Case for Christ movie

Some people need more tangible evidence. Remember Jesus' disciple Thomas? He was one of the Twelve. He had been close to Jesus and had been taught truth straight from the Source. Yet, Thomas still struggled with doubt. After the crucifixion and resurrection, Jesus appeared to the disciples, but Thomas wasn't there. So he didn't believe it. Thomas needed to see the risen Lord with his own eyes. And guess what? Jesus gave him what he needed— Jesus appeared to Thomas and told him to touch the scars on his hands and his side, to stop doubting, and to believe (John 20:27).

Do you ever feel like Thomas—the testimony of others is great, but you need to see the truth for yourself?

Is it okay to ask God for evidence or for personal experience? Why or why not?

How should we balance that desire with Jesus' words to Thomas: "Blessed are those who have not seen and yet have believed" (John 20:29)?

Our challenge is to pursue all the avenues we can in order to discover spiritual truth, realizing that God's truth is not limited to the sources we prefer.

As you ask hard questions, patience must permeate your investigation. There will be times when the answers aren't obvious, when the truth is hard to discern, when your unanswered questions cause pain and doubt. But you can trust that God is there in the midst of your search.

When you struggle with these matters, you can pray the "doubter's prayer" like the father who took his son to Jesus to be healed in Mark 9:14–27. Honestly say, as he did, "I do believe; help me overcome my unbelief!" (verse

> "One must keep on pointing out that Christianity is a statement which, if false, is of no importance, and if true, of infinite importance. The one thing it cannot be is moderately important."
>
> —C. S. Lewis, God in the Dock[1]

24). Jesus answered the prayer and helped that man, and he'll help you as well.

Does belief mean the absence of all doubt? Definitely not. But as London challenged Strobel, we can't use our doubts or fears as smoke screens to hide behind. We must face them and move forward. And as we pursue truth, we must engage our toughest questions and deepest doubts and allow God to strengthen our beliefs through them.

3. Embark on Your Journey

What is standing in the way of you believing in Christ? Or what's blocking you from engaging with him on a deeper level?

There are many obstacles that get in our way. Maybe you feel you can't believe without more information. Or maybe you just don't want to believe because you know it will interfere with your lifestyle. Perhaps you don't know fully what to believe—or you believe but wonder what's next. Or, probably for most of us, we do believe but feel the need to go deeper in our understanding, both for our own faith and for the sake of helping others. Wherever you are today, you can embark on a journey to investigate the Case for Christ.

Four Spiritual Sticking Points

Sticking Point	How to Get Unstuck
I *can't* believe.	Wholeheartedly seek God and the evidence for the claims of Christ.
I don't *want* to believe.	Weigh what you're hanging onto versus what you could gain by following Christ.
I don't know *what* to believe.	Read the Bible with an open mind, seeking to understand its central gospel message.
I do believe; isn't that *enough*?	Believing is the important first step. Now you need to receive the forgiveness and leadership of Christ.

As you investigate truth, you'll find that at some point you will face a decision. Just like Strobel was challenged by London in today's movie clip, we all reach a point where we have to face the truth we've learned and decide what we'll do about it.

When the evidence is in, will you act? Coming to the point of believing in God is good, but the journey doesn't stop there. A general intellectual agreement isn't enough. You can't learn to ride a bicycle simply by believing a bike exists. You must grab hold of the handlebars and take your feet off the ground as you learn to ride.

John 1:12 says, "As many as received Him, to them He gave the right to become children of God, even to those who believe in His name" (NASB). This verse spells it out simply and clearly: Believe + Receive = Become.

Pursuing truth until we believe in God is the beginning, but to become God's children, we must receive Jesus' offer of forgiveness, salvation, and leadership in our lives.

Are you ready to climb on the bike and ride?

APPLY

Continue this section together as time allows, or dig deeper on your own throughout the week.

Takeaway: God's truth is worth seeking with all your heart, no matter the obstacles.

Insights: What were you most encouraged or challenged by in this lesson? Use the space below to write down some personal reflections.

Action: On a scale of 1 to 10, rate your current relationship to God. One means "I don't believe God exists." Five means "I just received Jesus' gift of forgiveness and leadership." Ten means "I'm completely secure in God's truth and understand what and why I believe concerning the Case for Christ." Or you might be somewhere between those options.

1 2 3 4 5 6 7 8 9 10

I don't
believe
God exists.

I just received
Jesus' gift of
forgiveness
and leadership.

I'm completely
secure in God's
truth and
understand what
and why I believe
concerning the
Case for Christ.

Mark your answer and explain why you chose it. Also write down your biggest questions and the obstacles that get in the way of your search for answers.

Take some time to talk to God. If you're below 5 on the 1 to 10 scale, ask him to reveal himself to you and to lead you to the information and help you'll need to put your trust in him. If you're right on the cusp of taking that #5 step, then tell him you *believe* but now want to *receive* his forgiveness and leadership in your life so you can *become* his child (and be sure to tell your group leader you took this step!). And if you're on the upper end of the 1 to 10 scale, then ask him to keep deepening your understanding and faith so you can more confidently share it with others.

Q&A WITH LEE STROBEL, FROM *THE CASE FOR CHRIST ANSWER BOOKLET*[4]

I have so many questions—and a few doubts—about the Christian faith. What should I do with them?

You are doing precisely what you need to do—you're being honest with yourself and open with your questions. That's the first step toward finding answers. If you do the opposite—bottling up your concerns in the hopes they'll go away—then they'll just fester and infect your entire spiritual life.

Instead, let me urge you to follow the wisdom of Scripture. Jesus said, "Everyone who asks receives; the one who seeks finds; and to the one who knocks, the door will be opened" (Matthew 7:8). This echoes a principle in the Old Testament: "You will seek me and find me when you seek me with all your heart" (Jeremiah 29:13).

I've struggled with spiritual questions for most of my life, and in some ways I still do. It's an ongoing process to find answers that satisfy my heart and soul. But even bouts of doubt can show we're thinking and growing, rather than simply clinging to what we've been told.

As I described in *The Case for Christ*, my greatest season of spiritual introspection came after my wife, Leslie, announced that she had become a Christian. That was hard news for a skeptical journalist to hear! But it set in motion my own journey of asking tough questions—and discovering unexpected answers. In the end, I concluded that it would take more faith for me to maintain my atheism than it would to become a Christian!

After almost two years of searching, I got on my knees and asked Jesus to forgive my sins and lead my life. It was a decision that changed everything; in fact, it was the pivotal moment of my life.

That decision, mixed with the research I did then and in the time since then, led me to a sense of confidence that there are satisfying answers to even our hardest questions.

> *Jesus stayed behind . . . sitting among the teachers, listening to them and asking them questions. Everyone who heard him was amazed at his understanding and his answers. (Luke 2:43, 46–47)*

No. 651

Reporter's
Note Book

LESSON 2
Exploring the
Evidence for Christ

NOTES FROM

GET STARTED

Big Idea: Jesus really did live, die, and then rise again.

Icebreaker: Get the Picture

Leader's Note: Before you meet with your group, cut out some pictures from a magazine. Choose scenes, logos, or buildings that are recognizable to most people. Then cut off a significant portion of the picture so the image is barely identifiable. Save both parts of each image. Teams can have any number of people, so decide on a natural division for your group and have enough images so each team gets five to seven incomplete pictures.

Divide the group into teams. Hand one set of partial images to each team. Set the timer for one minute and see how many images each team can identify correctly.

Which image was easiest to identify and why? Which was hardest?

How many did your team get correct? What were the biggest clues? What threw you off?

Did everyone agree on every image?

Now put the partial images in a pile in the middle of the meeting space and see how long it takes the teams to match each of their images with its other part to create a whole picture.

How is this process similar to exploring evidence for something such as the existence of God or the resurrection of Jesus?

In life and faith, we don't always start with the whole picture—but we can look for clues and piece together information until the picture becomes clear.

WATCH

Video 2: Exploring the Evidence for Christ [DVD]

Setup: Strobel has been pursuing every angle he can to find a way to undermine Christianity. He has prodded and attacked the death of Jesus by crucifixion, the empty tomb, the accuracy of the eyewitnesses who saw him alive again, and the resurrection itself. He has traveled to meet with experts in each field and demanded sources outside the Bible itself. But he has hidden his investigation from his boss and his wife, and he has become volatile with his family due to his frustration and anger about Leslie's faith. He has become obsessed.

Recap: Now Strobel has traveled from Chicago to California to meet with Dr. Alexander Metherell. Perhaps he can find a way to prove Jesus wasn't really dead on the cross. And if he didn't die, he couldn't have been raised from the dead. It's the swoon theory, and Metherell has heard it before. He walks Strobel through the brutalities involved in a Roman crucifixion and the medical effects of each step of their torture. When Strobel questions Dr. Metherell's impartiality—because the doctor is a believer—Dr. Metherell refers him to an impartial source: the *Journal of the Amer-*

ican *Medical Associ-*
ation. Strobel reads
from the respected
scientific journal:
"Clearly the weight
of the medical
and historical ev-
idence indicates

> "There is nothing in time or eternity more absolutely certain and irrefutable than what Jesus Christ accomplished on the Cross—He made it possible for the entire human race to be brought back into a right-standing relationship with God."
>
> —Oswald Chambers, *My Utmost for His Highest*

that Jesus was dead before the wound to his side was in-
flicted. Accordingly, interpretations based on the assump-
tion that Jesus did not die on the cross appear to be at odds
with modern medical knowledge." This is not at all what
Strobel had hoped to hear.

DISCUSS

Read through each of the following sections and discuss
the questions together.

1. Trustworthy Sources

How important is the scientific conclusion from the *Jour-*
nal of the American Medical Association that Jesus truly
died by crucifixion?

In the video clip, Strobel chides Dr. Metherell for having a point of view—a bias toward Christian beliefs. But he seems blind to his own bias *against* those beliefs. Is there anyone who doesn't have some kind of a bias?

Once you realize what your bias is on any subject, is it possible to somehow compensate for that bias? Can you give an example of where you did so, or saw someone else do so successfully? Why is it important to try?

Is it fair to discount someone's testimony about a given event just because you know that person believes something about it? More specifically, what would you say to someone who discounts the reports of eyewitnesses of Jesus' crucifixion and resurrection just because those people are followers of Jesus?

Putting yourself in the shoes of the early disciples, can you imagine seeing Jesus die, and then three days later seeing him again after he had come back to life—and *not* being his follower?

The New Testament Gospels record a number of eyewitness accounts of Jesus' life, death, and resurrection. And those events formed the foundation of the church in Acts.

Are there differences in the Gospel accounts that bother you? They bothered Strobel. He spent a lot of time finding and pointing out anything he considered to be discrepancies. Yet he couldn't deny that the main events were the same. The core of the accounts was consistent—and for an investigative journalist, that is strong evidence. And that core message is what got passed on from the eyewitnesses to the thousands who formed the early church.

Can you think of an example in your life, or maybe in

"We could provide a broad outline of most of the major facts of Jesus' life from secular history alone. Such is surely significant. . . . We conclude that ancient extrabiblical sources provide a broad outline of the life of Jesus and indicate that he died due to the effects of crucifixion. Afterwards he was buried, and his tomb was later found empty."

—Gary Habermas, *The Historical Jesus* [2]

the news, where seemingly contradictory reports ended up both being true?

How do minor variations in the Gospel accounts—or in any eyewitness account—actually point to the authenticity of the reports? For example, how would a detective respond if three or four witnesses each gave an identical, verbatim account of an event?

One of the reasons people believe Jesus rose from the dead is because his tomb was empty. What kinds of evidence could you give to support this fact?

Matthew 28:12–13 reports that after Jesus' disappearance from the tomb, the chief priests met with the elders and devised a plan. They gave the soldiers a large sum of money and told them, "You are to say, 'His disciples came during the night and stole him away while we were asleep.'"

What do you make of their story? Do you think anyone believed it? Does their excuse even make sense? How does their story inadvertently *support* the resurrection claims of the Christians?

What would you say to someone who believes in God but doesn't think a miracle like Jesus' resurrection could even be possible? Would a resurrection be hard for a God who could create the universe out of nothing?

In his first letter to the Corinthians, Paul wrote,

> For what I received I passed on to you as of
> first importance: that Christ died for our sins
> according to the Scriptures, that he was bur-
> ied, that he was raised on the third day accord-
> ing to the Scriptures, and that he appeared to
> Cephas, and then to the Twelve. After that,
> he appeared to more than five hundred of the
> brothers and sisters at the same time, most of
> whom are still living, though some have fallen
> asleep. Then he appeared to James, then to all
> the apostles, and last of all he appeared to me
> also, as to one abnormally born.
>
> For I am the least of the apostles and
> do not even deserve to be called an apos-
> tle, because I persecuted the church of God.
> (1 Corinthians 15:3–9)

What's fascinating is that this is probably the earliest eyewitness report of these events, going back to within just a few years—and possibly even a few months—of the death and resurrection of Jesus!

Why are these early eyewitnesses that the passage describes so hard to discount or ignore? Does the fact that they were willing to die for their belief in the risen Jesus add to their credibility?

"The evidence confirms that the Jesus of history is the same person as the Christ of our faith. You can bet your life on it!"

—Lee Strobel, Today's Moment of Truth[3]

Have you ever thought about how Paul, the enemy of the church and persecutor of Christians, was so completely changed after what he claimed was an encounter with Christ on the road to Damascus? What would cause him to give up his status and prestige as a Pharisee to endure persecution, imprisonment, and countless other hardships—if not, as he claimed, that he had met the risen Christ?

Could you use the example of Paul's bold conversion as evidence when talking to a skeptical friend? What other reasons could you give for your beliefs about Christ?

What aspects of your faith, and the evidence that supports it, do you feel the need to study further? (Don't miss the recommended resources in the Dig Deeper section later in this lesson.)

2. The Questions of *Why?* . . . and *So What?*

When we reach the point where we believe the evidence for Jesus and his death on our behalf, two natural questions emerge: *Why?* and *So what?*

"Why would he do it? Why allow himself to be killed if he really is the Son of God? Why not use his power to defend himself?"

Those are the questions Strobel asked of the priest as they stood together staring at the Shroud of Turin in *The Case for Christ* movie. The answer he got in the film, and the answer we get in God's Word, is *love*. Jesus' life, death, and resurrection were all because of his love for us. In fact, the entire Bible is the unfolding story of God's amazing love for his people. John 3:16 is one of the best-known verses in the Bible for a reason—it answers this question of why. "For God so loved the world that he gave his one and only Son, that whoever believes in him shall not perish but have eternal life."

And then we are left with the question of "So what?" Does it really make any difference in my life whether the story of Jesus is true? Here are some examples of the differences it can make (adapted from *The Case for Christ* book):

- If Jesus is God's Son, his teachings aren't just good ideas; they are divine insights on which I can confidently build my life.

- If Jesus really lived life here on earth, he understands my pain, and if he rose from the dead, he is still alive and available for me to encounter and live in relationship with.

- If Jesus conquered death, he can give me the gift of eternal life.

- If Jesus is who he says he is, he deserves every bit of my commitment, obedience, and worship.[4]

Which of these implications most resonates with you?

What other answers to the question of "So what?" can you think of?

If all this is really true, how does it change what you should do today?

James 1:5 says, "If any of you lacks wisdom, you should ask God, who gives generously to all without finding fault, and it will be given to you."

3. Can You Believe It?

If you can answer the questions of whether Jesus' story is true, why he did it, and why it matters, do any questions remain? Perhaps the most important one: *Can you believe it?*

The evidence is there, and it points strongly toward the truth of Christianity. The Bible tells us what is required of us in Romans 10:9: "If you declare with your mouth, 'Jesus is Lord,' and believe in your heart that God raised him from the dead, you will be saved."

"Now what were unbelieving Jews saying in response to the disciples' proclamation that Jesus was risen? . . . They were saying, 'The disciples stole away His body.' The Jewish authorities did not deny the empty tomb but instead entangled themselves in a hopeless series of absurdities trying to explain it away. In other words, the Jewish claim that the disciples had stolen the body presupposes that the body was missing."

—William Lane Craig, On Guard[5]

Have you taken that step yet and told God that you believe and you want to receive him and his salvation? Is there any reason you wouldn't want to take that step today?

Hebrews 11:1 says, "Now faith is confidence in what we hope for and assurance about what we do not see."

APPLY

Continue this section together as time allows, or dig deeper on your own throughout the week.

Takeaway: The reality of God's love, shown by Jesus' death and resurrection, changes everything.

Insights: What were you most encouraged or challenged by in this lesson? Use the space below to write down some personal reflections.

Action: Write down the questions you still have and need answers to. Then start reading one of the books recommended in the Dig Deeper section in this chapter. Or call a Christian friend, pastor, or professor this week and discuss your questions and next spiritual steps. Along the way, talk to God about it. Ask him for wisdom to discern truth and grace to trust and follow Christ.

DIG DEEPER

Here are some recommended resources for further exploration of the evidence:

The Case for Christ, Lee Strobel (Zondervan, 1998, 2016)

The Case for Christ Study Guide with DVD: A Six-Session Investigation of the Evidence for Jesus, Lee Strobel and Garry Poole (Zondervan, 2014)

The Case for Christ Answer Book, Lee Strobel (Zondervan, 2014)

In Defense of Jesus, Lee Strobel (formerly *The Case for the Real Jesus*) (Zondervan, 2007, 2016)

The Case for Faith, Lee Strobel (Zondervan, 2000)

Today's Moment of Truth, Lee Strobel and Mark Mittelberg (Zondervan, 2016)

Confident Faith, Mark Mittelberg (Tyndale, 2013)

More Than a Carpenter, Josh McDowell and Sean McDowell (Tyndale, 2009)

Evidence for the Resurrection, by Josh McDowell and Sean McDowell (Regal, 2009)

The Case for the Resurrection of Jesus, Gary Habermas and Michael Licona (Kregel, 2004)

Cold-Case Christianity, J. Warner Wallace (David C Cook, 2013)

On Guard, William Lane Craig (David C Cook, 2010)

Q&A WITH LEE STROBEL, FROM *THE CASE FOR CHRIST ANSWER BOOKLET*[6]

What difference does it make today that a man rose from the dead two thousand years ago?

I once wondered the same thing—but soon realized the implications of Jesus' resurrection were huge. Here are three examples:

The resurrection establishes Jesus' identity.

After being asked by the Pharisees for some kind of proof that he was who he claimed to be, Jesus said in Matthew 12:39–40, "A wicked and adulterous generation asks for a sign! But none will be given it except the sign of the prophet Jonah. For as Jonah was three days and three nights in the belly of a huge fish, so the Son of Man will be three days and three nights in the heart of the earth." Jesus made it clear that the ultimate validation of his claims would be his own death, burial, and resurrection. These would show that he truly was the Son of God.

The resurrection validates the Christian faith.

This point flows from the last one. As the unique Son of God, Jesus is "calling God his own Father, making himself equal with God" (John 5:18). This validates the Christian doctrine of the Trinity—one God in three persons—Father, Son, and Holy Spirit. And because Jesus is God, he is also Lord, so we need to believe and obey him (Luke 6:46; Matthew 28:20).

The resurrection energizes the gospel message.

Jesus came "to give his life as a ransom for many" (Matthew 20:28). Paul explains this further: "He was delivered over to death for our sins and was raised to life for our justification" (Romans 4:25). Both elements are key to the gospel: Jesus' death made the necessary payment; Jesus' resurrection enabled him to apply that payment and to give us life. He has provided everything. All we need to do is say yes, and to follow him as our forgiver and leader.

> But Christ has indeed been raised from the dead, the firstfruits of those who have fallen asleep. For since death came through a man, the resurrection of the dead comes also through a man. For as in Adam all die, so in Christ all will be made alive. (1 Corinthians 15:20-22)

No. 651

Reporter's
Note Book

LESSON 3
Embracing the Truth of Christ

NOTES FROM _____ TO _____

GET STARTED

Big Idea: We embrace the truth by receiving Christ into our lives.

Icebreaker: Who Done It?

Leader's Note: Each person in your group will need a copy of the *Who Done It?* page at the end of this lesson (page 64). If any of your group members do not have a copy of this study guide, please copy that page for them before your meeting.

Using the *Who Done It?* list of activities—traveled to Paris, spent the night under the stars, invited a stranger to coffee, piloted a plane, etc.—each person must ask around in the group to see who has done what. When you find someone who has done one of the activities, have that person sign his or her name on the line next to it.

After giving the group a few minutes to interact and collect signatures, bring them back together and talk about what they discovered.

What was the most commonly completed activity?

Were there any activities on the list that nobody in the group had ever tried?

How many items on the list were things you've imagined doing, or even intend to try at some point?

Note that the only person who could sign your paper is someone who has actually been there, done that—they're someone *Who Done It!*

We all have mental lists of things we think would be fun or meaningful in our lives, but we often fail to try the activity or go to the place in our dreams. This is true in the spiritual realm, as well. Many people acknowledge that following Christ would be the best way to live but stop short of acting on that belief by embracing him as their leader.

In today's session we'll talk about how we can move beyond mere belief and really embrace Jesus as our forgiver and the leader of our lives.

WATCH

Video 3: Embracing the Truth of Christ [DVD]

Setup: Lee Strobel has exhausted his investigation over the last few months. He has pursued all the theories he could find to debunk Jesus and Christianity. He has talked to experts and scholars. He has read books and journals on both sides of the arguments. He has thrown his investigative reporting skills into this search with all he's got. At the same time, he has hurt his wife emotionally, and their relationship has suffered. Finally, he has followed the facts and evidence and weighed the pros and cons. And what he has found is the exact opposite of what he set out to prove.

"My mind is convinced that it is true; my emotions have been deeply stirred; and now they both appeal to my will for a decision. To be true to my God and myself and my eternal future I have only one course open, and I must take it. Today I'll make Jesus Christ my forgiver and leader; my Savior and Lord."

—Robert A. Laidlaw, businessman[1]

Recap: Lee is finally ready to come clean with his wife, Leslie. As he sits down with her on the couch, Lee does what he never could have imagined—he tells Leslie that after trying to disprove Christianity, he's failed to do so. This is unexpected news for Leslie, and it is an emotional moment. "I believe," he tells her. Filled with emotion and still young in her own relationship with God, Leslie helps Lee understand the importance of not only believing the truth but also receiving Jesus into his life. She reads John 1:12 to him, drawing from the three active verbs in that verse: "But as many as received Him, to them He gave the right to become children of God, even to those who believe in His name" (NASB). And she explains what it means: Believe + Receive = Become. Lee is ready to receive Christ. Although he doesn't know exactly what to say, he prays and surrenders his life to God.

DISCUSS

What different levels of healing do you see taking place in this scene?

What stands out to you about Lee's prayer?

How is Lee's encounter with God in this scene similar or different from your own?

Read through each of the following lesson points and discuss the questions together.

1. The Pursuit

We often hear people talking about pursuing God. How many sermons have you heard or Bible studies have you done based on the theme of seeking God with your whole heart?

> "Whether our sins are subtle or spectacular, we all need grace. Fortunately, it's available to each of us through Christ."
>
> —Lee Strobel, *Today's Moment of Truth*[2]

Even this study guide has talked about it! But pursuing God is a mysterious adventure. While it is right for us to seek him, the more we try to find God, the more we realize he's been there all along. In fact, he initiated the pursuit! While we may feel at times like we are searching for God, he is the one who has been seeking us out from the start. Check out these verses:

> *But God demonstrates his own love for us in this: While we were still sinners, Christ died for us. (Romans 5:8)*

> *We love because he first loved us. (1 John 4:19)*

Who made the first move? Both verses point us back to God as the one initiating the first move. He didn't wait around for humankind to figure out the evidence or answer all the questions. He broke through to us and initiated a loving relationship with us through Jesus.

Also, Psalm 139 describes how intimately God knows each one of us. He knew us when we were formed in our mothers' wombs, and he knows our actions, thoughts, and words. He knows you, and he loves you! God didn't just send Jesus to die for the world; he sent Jesus to die for *you*.

Revelation 3:20 says, "Here I am! I stand at the door and knock. If anyone hears my voice and opens the door, I will come in and eat with that person, and they with me."

What does this verse tell you about God's availability to us? What does it tell you about God's desire to pursue you?

What evidence have you seen in your own life that God is pursuing you?

Right now, do you feel more like the pursuer or the pursued? Why?

2. God's Gift

What's the best gift you've ever received?

Why was it so special or so important to you? Was it more about the gift or the giver?

Jesus' life, death, and resurrection are the ultimate gift to us.[3] It's an expensive gift, paid for in full by God himself, which we don't deserve and could never earn—so we can't take credit for it or brag about it. And it's not just intended for a few religious elite. Quite the opposite! This gift is meant for all.

"But the gift is not like the trespass," says Romans 5:15,

"Ultimately, the way a Christian really knows that Christianity is true is through the self-authenticating witness of God's Spirit. The Holy Spirit whispers to our spirit that we belong to God. That's one of his roles. Other evidence, though still valid, is basically confirmatory."

—William Lane Craig, theologian[4]

> "There's no wrong way or right way. Just you—you talk to God. You tell him your heart. . . . Right here. Right now. This is church."
>
> —Leslie Strobel, The Case for Christ movie

referring to sin that entered the world through Adam. "For if the many died by the trespass of the one man, how much more did God's grace and the gift that came by the grace of the one man, Jesus Christ, overflow to the many!"

God, through Christ, has *done* everything necessary to provide and offer his gift of salvation. There is nothing we can do to earn it.

How do you feel about the free gift Jesus offers? Is it easy or hard for you to accept something that is free—something you can't earn no matter how hard you try?

If we can't earn it, then on a practical level how can we make this gift our own? We touched on it earlier in this study—it starts with believing in both the gift and the Giver.

Jesus said, "I am the way and the truth and the life. No one comes to the Father except through me" (John 14:6).

Talking to Martha after her brother, Lazarus, had died, Jesus said to her, "I am the resurrection and the life. The one who believes in me will live, even though they die; and whoever lives by believing in me will never die. Do you believe this?" (John 11:25–26).

How is it different to believe in the truth of evidence and facts versus believing in the person of Jesus?

What is the difference between *"believing that"* and *"believing in"*?

Is one more natural for you than the other? How do they go hand in hand?

"God, I have no idea what I'm doing, but I cannot ignore the evidence. . . . I believe it. I believe you. . . . I believe you're real. And I don't know what comes next. I don't know what it means. I just know that I want that. I want whatever's next. I want that. So let's do that. Amen."

—Lee Strobel, The Case for Christ movie

3. Our Response

What are we to do with all this? How do we respond both to the overwhelming evidence for the truth and to the gift of salvation offered to us in Jesus?

Fortunately, this question is answered in the words of John 1:12. This is the verse Lee Strobel's wife read to him in the movie clip when he was ready to commit his life to God. The verse says, "As many as received Him, to them He gave the right to become children of God, even to those who believe in His name" (NASB).

We've touched on this before, and Leslie Strobel described it briefly in the video clip we watched from the movie, but what three active verbs do you see in this verse?

Those three verbs form a "faith formula" that concisely presents what it takes for us to move beyond mere intellectual agreement into a personal relationship with Jesus: Believe + Receive = Become. Let's look at each part more deeply.

Believe

The formula starts with believe. The idea is that you can carefully check out Jesus' credentials in order to know that he is who he claimed to be and therefore merits your trust. This is the knowledge side of faith—coming to the point of confidence that Jesus really is the unique Son of God and Savior of the world.

Unfortunately, many people gain that knowledge but then stop cold. They nod their heads in agreement with the truth, but they never take the next step and express real faith. Many of them even go to church and become religious non-Christians. That's why we must go beyond merely believing to the second part of the equation.

+ Receive

In the devotional *Today's Moment of Truth* by Lee Strobel and Mark Mittelberg, Mittelberg illustrated this second element when he said,

> [Later] I'm heading to the airport to fly back home. But it's not enough for me to sit in the terminal and believe *that* airplanes fly. Just acknowledging the soundness of aviation science will never get me home. I have to go beyond mere belief that airplanes fly to a personal belief *in* the particular airplane that's heading to my city—demonstrated by climbing on board. It's that act of trust that will ultimately get me where I want to go.[5]

So genuine faith goes beyond just nodding its head to the theory of flight; it puts that belief into action by climbing on board an airplane and actually going somewhere. Similarly, Scripture tells us we need to not only *believe* the truth about Jesus, but we also must *receive* him and what he offers us. This is how we gain the gift of salvation—by humbly admitting our need for it and asking God for his forgiveness and leadership.

Like a gift that is offered at Christmas, you have to reach out and receive it. To do so is not to earn anything; receiving a gift is not the same as working for it. God is offering you his gift of salvation. All that's left for you to do is reach out and take it. If you refuse to do so, then the gift will not be yours. But if you'll humbly accept that gift, then it will be your own.

= Become

The third element in the formula is *become*. The Bible makes it clear that when we sincerely believe in the claims of Jesus and receive him as our forgiver and leader, then at that moment we are cleansed of all our sins, and we become God's adopted sons and daughters.

That simple step is what it takes to become a true Christian—a forgiven child of God. And what comes after that? It's a life of adventure as you follow and serve him, doing, as it says in Ephesians 2:10, "the good things he planned for us" (NLT). That's not a way to try to pay for or earn what you've already been given; it's an expression of love and gratitude to the one who freely gave it to you.

> "Jesus answered, 'I am the way and the truth and the life. No one comes to the Father except through me.'"
>
> —John 14:6

How about you? Do you *believe*? Will you *receive* as well? His ways are the best ways for you—he loves you, and he wants to forgive you and guide you into becoming all that he made you to be. Believing and receiving are the only path to becoming a true son or daughter of God.

But what if you've already believed and received God's gift of salvation? Is this all irrelevant to you? Of course not. Living in relationship with God is a continual process of growing and learning. God is always at work in the lives of his children to bring them closer to him. As you face challenges to your faith or struggle with doubts about aspects of what you believe, the same basic principles of *Believe + Receive = Become* apply in order to draw you deeper into relationship with God.

Paul wrote, "Therefore, my dear friends, as you have always obeyed—not only in my presence, but now much more in my absence—continue to work out your salvation with fear and trembling, for it is God who works in you to will and to act in order to fulfill his good purpose" (Philippians 2:12–13).

How did you first believe?

When did you receive Jesus as your Savior?

How has your life changed since then?

APPLY

Continue this section together as time allows, or dig deeper on your own throughout the week.

Takeaway: Embracing God's truth leads us into a real and deepening relationship with him as we believe and receive his gift of life.

Insights: What were you most encouraged or challenged by in this lesson? Use the space on the next page to write down some personal reflections.

Action: Where are you on your journey of investigating Christ? Have you believed his truth? Have you received his gift of life? Is there an area of your life where you still need to surrender, or need to surrender again, to him as Lord?

If you are ready to receive God's gift of salvation for the first time, talk to someone in your group. There is no official prayer that you must pray. Like Strobel in the movie, you can talk honestly with God, expressing in your own words your desire to receive his forgiveness and guidance in your life.

If you've already received God's salvation, talk to him about any area of your life you need to surrender and receive his forgiveness and restoration.

Whatever step you take today, carve out time this week to record your thoughts, your feelings, and the events that have led you to this point. Whether you write it in a journal, sketch a picture, create a painting, or compose a song, make something meaningful that will help you remember this time. It will serve as an important marker in your life and your relationship with God.

Q&A WITH LEE STROBEL, FROM *THE CASE FOR CHRIST ANSWER BOOKLET*[6]

Jesus did many things, but what was his real mission?

Jesus—who was God incarnate—came for a very specific reason. He explained in Mark 10:45, "For even the Son of Man did not come to be served, but to serve, and to give his life as a ransom for many."

Why would Jesus talk in terms of making a payment to release captives? The answer is *we're all captives to sin.* And because of our sin we've incurred a debt we can't afford to pay. Romans 6:23 explains, "The wages of sin is death." This means we deserve a spiritual death penalty—one we'll have to pay for all eternity.

Thankfully, Jesus came to die on the cross to pay our ransom and set us free. He "suffered once for sins, the righteous for the unrighteous, to bring you to God" (1 Peter 3:18). This means Jesus paid the death penalty in our place. That's why Romans 6:23 ends with "but the gift of God is eternal life in Christ Jesus our Lord." No wonder the gospel is called Good News!

But some people ask why God couldn't simply forgive people without sacrificing his Son. In response, philosopher Paul Copan, in our interview for *The Case for the Real Jesus*, points to the parable in Matthew 18:21-35, which describes a king who forgives a great debt.

"Notice what happens in that parable. The king doesn't just forgive," Copan explains. "He also absorbs the debt. The king basically says he's going to bear the burden of the loss even though the servant owes him money. Similarly, Jesus paid the cost of our sin on the cross. It's like a child who breaks a neighbor's window. He may be too young to pay the price himself, so his parents pay it for him."

We're like the servant—or the child. Thankfully God, in Christ, assumed and absorbed our debt. He paid our ransom in order to set captives like us—you and me—free for eternity.

> *Here is a trustworthy saying that deserves full acceptance: Christ Jesus came into the world to save sinners—of whom I am the worst.*
> *(1 Timothy 1:15)*

WHO DONE IT?

Ask the people in your group what activities they've done. Collect signatures of people who have done any of the activities listed on this page. See how many signatures you can get filled in. Try to gather a different signature for each activity, or set a limit based on your group size for how many activities one person can sign for.

Traveled to Paris _____

Spent the night under the stars _____

Invited a stranger to coffee _____

Piloted a plane _____

Met the president _____

Learned to swim _____

Completed a marathon _____

Played a band instrument _____

Learned a new language _____

Donated money to a charity _____

Visited all fifty states _____

Climbed a mountain _____

Read the entire Bible _____

Attended the Olympics _____

Sent a love letter _____

Gave birth to a child _____

Drove coast to coast _____

Completed a college degree _____

Mentored a child _____

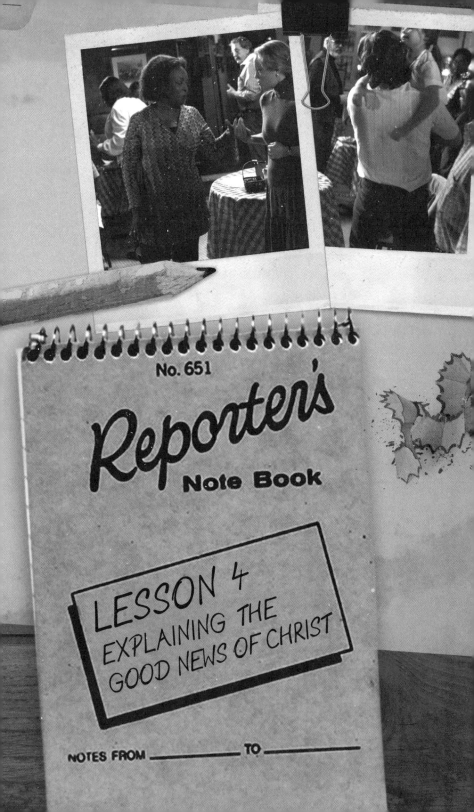

GET STARTED

Big Idea: God invites us to share the Good News of Jesus with others.

Icebreaker: Word Match

Leader's Note: Write the words below on note cards or strips of paper, one word per card. Make two complete sets. Be sure to have a way to keep time—the timer on your phone will work well.

- surprise

- adventure

- opportunity

- conversation

- listen

- truth

- answers

- become

- risk

- friend

- relationship

- love

Divide your group into two teams. Each team gets a set of cards but cannot look at them. Set the timer for one minute. One person draws a card and tries to get their team to guess the word. The prompter can talk and use

> "I'm not saying that people will become Christians because of the arguments and evidence. Rather I'm saying that the arguments and evidence will help to create a culture in which Christian belief is a reasonable thing."
>
> —William Lane Craig, On Guard[1]

any words or actions, but he or she cannot say any form of the actual word. Once the team guesses the word, the next person on the team draws a card and tries to get the team to guess that word. See how many of the twelve words each team can guess in one minute. Depending on the progress of the teams, you can stop after one minute or play another round.

After the final round, talk about the game.

What were the easiest words to guess?

Who was best at prompting the team? Who was best at guessing?

Did anyone notice that some people in the group were pretty reserved when we first described this game? In fact, some of you could probably *feel* it—that not everyone wanted to participate at first. But then, you each spoke up and ventured a guess . . . and then another and another, until you were totally caught up in it. You came out of your shell, to the point that, when our time was up, it was hard to get some of you to stop talking!

That's often the way it is; we start out being reluctant to interact, whether in a game or a conversation—but then, once the ice is broken, we realize we're really enjoying it. In fact, once we get going, it can be hard to quit! Well, the same is true when it comes to explaining the Good News of Christ to others. We tend to be reluctant at first, but once we get into it, we realize it's quite exhilarating. But in order to get to that place of excitement, we often have to force ourselves to take the first step.

Note: This final session is geared primarily for those who have received Christ and want to communicate their faith to others. If you haven't yet put your faith in Christ, please participate as much as possible, but don't feel obligated to practice telling your story later in the session. Instead, you might want to sit in with another pair and listen as they both share theirs. Or you might tell someone in the group your story so far, and gain encouragement from them about next steps you can take in your journey toward faith.

WATCH

Video 4: Explaining the Good News of Christ [DVD]

Setup: Lee Strobel has just received an award and a promotion for his investigative journalism at the *Chicago*

> Alfie: How did you reach Lee in the past?
>
> Leslie: We'd talk, I guess. We used to really talk . . . and listen.
>
> Alfie: So do that.
>
> —The Case for Christ movie

Tribune. He has broken a big story on a corporate cover-up and established his reputation as a hot up-and-comer. Strobel is good, and he knows it. This calls for more celebration, so he and his young family go out to eat to do just that.

Recap: At the restaurant, Lee's daughter, Ali, chokes on a piece of candy. She can't breathe. Lee and Leslie try to help, but they can't. Precious seconds are slipping by, and the parents are desperate. They call out for help. Fortunately, a woman named Alfie steps in and saves their little girl. She says she's a nurse. And when Leslie expresses how lucky they are that she was around, Alfie responds, "It's not luck—it's Jesus. My husband and I were on our way to another restaurant tonight, but something told me I needed to be here."

DISCUSS

Do you believe in luck? Why or why not?

What do you think you would have done and said if you had been in Alfie's shoes? Why?

Read through each of the following lesson points and discuss the questions together.

1. Words of Life

Have you ever noticed that Jesus talked to pretty much everyone? It drove the religious leaders of his day crazy. He was always talking with people he wasn't supposed to associate with. But Jesus didn't live by their prejudices and rules. In John 4, he was up to it again. Sitting by a well at midday, he asked a Samaritan woman for a drink of water. Likely, he was actually thirsty, but he used an ordinary encounter to share the extraordinary news of who he was and why he had come.

The truth Jesus shared with this woman had the potential to change her life forever. Jesus said, "Everyone who drinks this water will be thirsty again, but whoever drinks the water I give them will never thirst. Indeed, the water I give them will become in them a spring of water welling up to eternal life" (John 4:13–14).

The Samaritan woman needed to hear words of life. Who do you know that needs to hear words of life? Are you willing to associate with that person and share time together? Are you prepared to explain the Good News of Jesus?

That's something God wants to do through all of his followers. After we *believe* the message of the gospel with our minds and *receive* with our hearts the offer of life in Christ, we *become* new creations in Christ. We become disciples of Jesus. We experience the process of being transformed as we live by the guidance of the Holy Spirit. And we become vessels for God's love and grace.

Jesus' final instructions to his disciples were, "Go into all the world and preach the gospel to all creation" (Mark 16:15; see also Matthew 28:18–20). The disciples had been learning from Jesus what it meant to follow him, and now they were told to take the message they had heard and share it with the world.

Peter added that we should "always be prepared to give an answer to everyone who asks

> "A person's coming to Christ is like a chain with many links. . . . There are many influences and conversations that precede a person's decision to convert to Christ. I know the joy of being the first link at times, a middle link usually, and occasionally the last link. God has not called me to only be the last link. He has called me to be faithful and to love all people."
>
> —Cliffe Knechtle, evangelist [2]

you to give the reason for the hope that you have. But do this with gentleness and respect" (1 Peter 3:15).

In *Today's Moment of Truth*, Lee Strobel talked about preparing to explain the Good News. "God wants you to be his winsome representative. Do what it takes to get ready. Know what you believe and why, and learn how to say it in plain language. Then 'make the most of every opportunity' to tell others about Christ."[3]

Often the best way to present the message of Christ is to share your own story of God's transformative work in your life.

What is your spiritual story? Jot down an outline below.

Note: You may want to use the simple outline that Mark Mittelberg and Lee Strobel teach in the Becoming a Contagious Christian *training course:*[4]

- BC: What was your life like before you became a Christian?

- Christ: What did you learn about him, and how did you receive him?

- AD: Since meeting him, how has he changed your life?

Take a few minutes in your group to pair off and briefly tell each other the story of how you came to believe the Good News, receive the salvation of Christ, and become a child of God. Consider this to be part of the preparation 1 Peter 3:15 commands to every Christian, so we'll be able to effectively proclaim and defend Jesus' message with those who don't know him.

Next, while we're in pairs, briefly practice telling each other the faith formula that flows out of John 1:12: "As many as received Him, to them He gave the right to become children of God, even to those who believe in His name" (NASB)—Believe + Receive = Become. It's simple, but it can be powerful in helping people understand and embrace the grace of God through Christ.

In our hurried world, we are more and more disconnected from the people we live right next to. While we need to prepare the words we'd like to say, we also must carve out the time needed to do so.

What steps can you take to foster a lifestyle that leaves room for prayer, welcoming neighbors, and having meaningful conversations with them?

Is there purposeful space and opportunity in your church to allow people to ask deep questions and seek meaningful answers? How might you be part of creating or deepening that culture?

Not everyone will be open to hearing, and that's okay. Our call is to be faithful with the opportunities that arise, because as the apostle Paul explained, there are many people who need to hear the message from us—Jesus' followers—in order to believe: "But how can they call on him to save them unless they believe in him? And how can they believe in him if they have never heard about him? And how can they hear about him unless someone tells them?" (Romans 10:14, NLT).

2. Love in Action

As important as words can be in explaining the Good News, Jesus didn't rely on words alone. Jesus didn't just *say* he loved people; he *showed* it. Jesus served the blind by restoring their sight. He served lepers by restoring their health. And in the ultimate act of servanthood, Jesus gave his life to pay for the sins of the world.

John explained it this way:

> *This is how we know what love is: Jesus Christ*
> *laid down his life for us. And we ought to lay*
> *down our lives for our brothers and sisters.*
> *If anyone has material possessions and sees*
> *a brother or sister in need but has no pity*
> *on them, how can the love of God be in that*
> *person? Dear children, let us not love with*
> *words or speech but with actions and in truth.*
> *(1 John 3:16–18)*

What are the trademarks of someone who is genuinely loving toward others—as the verse puts it, both with actions and in truth?

How can you imitate the love of Christ by putting love into action toward others this week? Can you share a specific example of something you might do?

In *The Unexpected Adventure*, Lee Strobel referred to our "compassion radar," which needs to always be engaged.[5] That radar keeps us aware of the hurt and needs of others. Sometimes the most loving thing we can do is simply to recognize and acknowledge the need in someone else's life.

What does the Bible have to say about putting love into action? It tells us: "Religion that God our Father accepts as pure and faultless is this: to look after orphans and widows in their distress and to keep oneself from being polluted by the world" (James 1:27). And it tells us the way the world will know we are followers of Christ is by our love: "By this everyone will know that you are my disciples, if you love one another" (John 13:35).

Paul also admonished us as Christians to "be wise in the way you act toward outsiders; make the most of every opportunity. Let your conversation be always full of grace, seasoned with salt, so that you may know how to answer everyone" (Colossians 4:5–6).

What needs do you see in the lives of the people around you?

What steps can you take to help meet those needs?

How can you create enough margin in your daily life and routine to notice and engage with the needs of others?

3. Joining God's Work

When you look at the needs in your own life, in your community, and around the world, do you ever feel overwhelmed? Sometimes it's tough to just get through the day, let alone share words of life and put love in action toward others.

But this is perhaps where we miss the beauty and the mystery. Sharing the Good News doesn't have to be overwhelming, because it's God's work not ours. God needs our willingness to join him, not our skill or perfection. He wants to work through us. And we can take comfort in this promise he gives us: "My grace is sufficient for you, for my power is made perfect in weakness" (2 Corinthians 12:9).

> "The most powerful reason for jumping into the unexpected adventure of evangelism is because people matter to God, and therefore they should matter to us."
> —Lee Strobel, *The Unexpected Adventure* [6]

At a loss for words? His Spirit will guide you. "What we have received is not the spirit of the world, but the Spirit who is from God, so that we may understand what God has freely given us. This is what we speak, not in words taught us by human wisdom but in words taught by the Spirit, explaining spiritual realities with Spirit-taught words" (1 Corinthians 2:12–13).

And it's okay not to have all the answers! Even great theologians and scholars don't have answers for everything. Instead of letting that become an obstacle, allow it to be an invitation to explore deeper. What can we say if someone asks a question we don't know how to respond to?

"When someone raises an objection to Christianity that you can't answer, the best response isn't to sputter or sulk, to get flustered or angry, or to make up an explanation just so you have something to say," wrote Mark Mittelberg in *The Unexpected Adventure*. "Tell the person with sincerity that you simply don't know, and then invite him or her to pursue the answers with you." [7]

In the movie clip, we saw how Alfie's willingness to follow God's leading not only allowed her to save Ali's

> "For I am not ashamed of the gospel, because it is the power of God that brings salvation to everyone who believes: first to the Jew, then to the Gentile."
>
> —Romans 1:16

life but also to be part of the process of Leslie (and eventually Lee) beginning a relationship with Christ. She simply listened to God's nudge to eat dinner at a particular restaurant. She showed up and was available for God to work through her.

Do you remember the story in the Bible of Philip and the Ethiopian? Acts 8:26 starts off the account of this story by saying, "Now an angel of the Lord said to Philip, 'Go south to the road—the desert road—that goes down from Jerusalem to Gaza.'" The very next phrase is "So he started out" (verse 27). Without hesitation, Philip followed God's direction and was then able to explain the meaning of the passage of Scripture that the Ethiopian was reading. As a result, that man believed in God and was baptized. Imagine if Philip had not been willing to join God on this unexpected adventure. That man may not have come to know Jesus that day—or possibly *ever*. And Philip certainly would have missed out on an incredible opportunity to serve God and impact the lives of people.

How does the prospect of proclaiming the message of Christ with your words, actions, and life make you feel?

What tends to keep you from doing this? Fear? Busyness? Your personality? Doubt?

Surrender any weaknesses you struggle with to God and ask him to show you where you can join in his work.

Being in the center of God's work is always the best place to be. It may be hard, but it is good. Sharing his Good News is intended to be part of the rich blessing of your relationship with him, not a burden. Becoming who he created you to be is part of the full and abundant life he said he has given you (John 10:10).

APPLY

Continue this section together as time allows, or dig deeper on your own throughout the week.

Takeaway: God wants to use us to help others believe his truth, receive his life, and become followers of him.

Insights: What were you most encouraged or challenged by in this lesson? Use the space below to write down some personal reflections.

Action: Outdoor hikers and adventurers often use a compass to direct them. The compass orients them and tells them which direction they should be headed. As we seek to share Christ's love with others, we trust God as our compass. He is the one who directs us and tells us what direction we should go.

Place some form of a compass in a location where it can serve as a frequent reminder to be open to God's unexpected adventures. Perhaps you can attach a miniature compass to your coat zipper, make a compass the homepage image on your computer or phone, hang one from the mirror in your car, place it on your desk, or attach it to your backpack. Choose a place where you'll see it often

> "Let's talk to God about our friends before we talk to our friends about God."
>
> —Mark Mittelberg, The Unexpected Adventure[8]

and be reminded to be open to where God wants to use you to share the Good News of Jesus. God knows where he is at work, he knows the hearts that are open to his love, and he knows who could use an encouraging or challenging word from us. Will you be open to joining him on unexpected adventures to share his message with others?

> *I consider my life worth nothing to me; my only aim is to finish the race and complete the task the Lord Jesus has given me—the task of testifying to the good news of God's grace. (Acts 20:24)*

Note: If your group would like to continue to meet and to go deeper in studying these themes, we'd recommend The Case for Christ Study Guide with DVD: A Six-Session Investigation of the Evidence for Jesus, *by Lee Strobel and Garry Poole (Zondervan, 2014).*

LESSON 4: Explaining the Good News of Christ 83

Q&A WITH LEE STROBEL, FROM *THE CASE FOR CHRIST ANSWER BOOK*[9]

Why are some Christians so adamant about telling everyone else about their faith? Shouldn't we just let people come to their own conclusions?

Often, we don't get any warning before a heart attack strikes, a drunk driver crosses the centerline, a wildfire or flood sweeps through a canyon, or an airplane loses power. So the question we're compelled to ask people is this: *"Are you ready?"*

One of the first verses I memorized as a Christian was 1 John 5:13: "I write these things to you who believe in the name of the Son of God so that you may know that you have eternal life." God doesn't want us to be wondering or steeped in anxiety over whether we're headed for heaven. He says we can *know*.

The Bible also makes it clear that we can be religious but not be in a right relationship with God. Religious activities and affiliations never saved anyone. Salvation comes from knowing Christ personally and receiving his provision for our sin. But it doesn't happen automatically. It doesn't come by attending a great church, being baptized, taking communion, or hanging out with a bunch of Christians. It comes from deciding to turn from your sins, to stop trusting in your own resources, and to accept the forgiveness and eternal life that Jesus purchased on the cross for you. *That* is how you gain God's peace and confidence.

At the risk of sounding overbearing, I want to tell everyone I can to settle it now, so that their eternity with God will be secure if tragedy were to strike. And if you haven't done so, or if you aren't sure that you have, I would urge you to receive the forgiveness and leadership of Christ right away as well.

Then you can know that even if the very worst thing were to happen to you today, it will immediately be followed by the very best thing of all.

> *For to me, to live is Christ and to die is gain. (Philippians 1:21)*

ENDNOTES

Lesson 1: Investigating the Case for Christ

1 C. S. Lewis, *The Quotable Lewis*, ed. Wayne Martindale and Jerry Root (Wheaton, IL: Tyndale, 1989), 49, https://books.google.com/books?id=f3mR0-_rUJQC&pg=PA49&dq=Christianity,+if+false,+is+of+no+importance,&hl=en&sa=X&ved=0ahUKEwjSzPH3sYLRAhXM7oMKHTqPBWEQ6AEILzAD#v=onepage&q=Christianity%2C%20if%20false%2C%20is%20of%20no%20importance%2C&f=false.

2 Lee Strobel, *The Case for Faith Student Edition* (Grand Rapids, MI: Youth Specialties, 2002), 79.

3 Lee Strobel, *The Case for Christ Answer Book* (Grand Rapids, MI: Zondervan, 2014), 5.

4 Lee Strobel, *The Case for Christ Answer Booklet* (Grand Rapids, MI: Zondervan, 2017), 1–2.

Lesson 2: Exploring the Evidence for Christ

1 Oswald Chambers, *My Utmost for His Highest*, ed. James Reimann, updated edition (Grand Rapids, MI: Discovery Books, 1992), "The Collision of God and Sin," April 6.

2 Gary R. Habermas, *The Historical Jesus* (Joplin, MO: College Press Publishing Company, 1996), 224–25.

3 Lee Strobel and Mark Mittelberg, *Today's Moment of Truth* (Grand Rapids, MI: Zondervan, 2016), 61.

4 Adapted from Lee Strobel, *The Case for Christ* (Grand Rapids, MI: Zondervan, 1998), 288.

5 William Lane Craig, *On Guard* (Colorado Springs, CO: David C Cook, 2010), 229.

6 Lee Strobel, *The Case for Christ Answer Booklet* (Grand Rapids, MI: Zondervan, 2017), 31–32.

Lesson 3: Embracing the Truth of Christ

1 Quoted in Mark Mittelberg, *The Reason Why* (Carol Stream, IL: Tyndale, 2011), 116.

2 Lee Strobel and Mark Mittelberg, *Today's Moment of Truth*

(Grand Rapids, MI: Zondervan, 2016), 96–97.

3   The following explanation, adapted slightly, is from Mark Mittelberg's *The Reason Why* (Carol Stream, IL: Tyndale, 2011), starting on page 106. It also incorporates some from the formula in Lee Strobel's *The Case for Christ* (Grand Rapids, MI: Zondervan, 1998), found on page 289.

4   William Lane Craig, interviewed by Lee Strobel, *The Case for Christ* (Grand Rapids, MI: Zondervan, 1998), 306.

5   Lee Strobel and Mark Mittelberg, *Today's Moment of Truth* (Grand Rapids, MI: Zondervan, 2016), 343.

6   Lee Strobel, *The Case for Christ Answer Booklet* (Grand Rapids, MI: Zondervan, 2017), 17–18.

Lesson 4: Explaining the Good News of Christ

1   William Lane Craig, *On Guard* (Colorado Springs, CO: David C Cook, 2010), 18.

2   Quoted in Lee Strobel and Mark Mittelberg, *The Unexpected Adventure* (Grand Rapids, MI: Zondervan, 2009), 109.

3   Lee Strobel and Mark Mittelberg, *Today's Moment of Truth* (Grand Rapids, MI: Zondervan, 2016), 191.

4   Mark Mittelberg, Lee Strobel, Bill Hybels, *Becoming a Contagious Christian Participant's Guide* (Grand Rapids, MI: Zondervan, 1995, 2007).

5   Lee Strobel and Mark Mittelberg, *The Unexpected Adventure* (Grand Rapids, MI: Zondervan, 2009), 61.

6   Lee Strobel and Mark Mittelberg, *The Unexpected Adventure* (Grand Rapids, MI: Zondervan, 2009), 274.

7   Lee Strobel and Mark Mittelberg, *The Unexpected Adventure* (Grand Rapids, MI: Zondervan, 2009), 28.

8   Lee Strobel and Mark Mittelberg, *The Unexpected Adventure* (Grand Rapids, MI: Zondervan, 2009), 131.

9   Lee Strobel, *The Case for Christ Answer Book* (Grand Rapids, MI: Zondervan, 2014), 194–196.

CHECK OUT THESE OTHER MOVIE STUDIES!